PRELUDES AND FUGUES

PRELUDES
AND FUGUES

Emmanuel Moses
Translated by Marilyn Hacker

Oberlin College Press
Oberlin, Ohio

Poems from *Sombre comme le temps* © 2014 Editions Gallimard, Paris.
Poems from *Préludes et fugues* © 2011 Editions Belin. Used by permission.

The FIELD Translation Series, vol. 32
Oberlin College Press, 50 N. Professor Street, Oberlin, OH 44074
www.oberlin.edu/ocpress

Cover image: *"Paysage urbain,"* painting by Liliane Klapisch.
Reproduced by permission of the artist.
Cover and book design: Steve Farkas.

Library of Congress Cataloging-in-Publication Data

Names: Moses, Emmanuel, 1960- author. | Hacker, Marilyn, 1942-
translator.
Title: Preludes and fugues / Emmanuel Moses ; translated by
Marilyn Hacker.
Description: Oberlin, Ohio : Oberlin College Press, [2016] | Series: The
FIELD Translation Series ; Vol. 32
Identifiers: LCCN 2015044423| ISBN 9780932440938 (pbk. : alk. paper) |
ISBN 0932440932 (pbk. : alk. paper)
Classification: LCC PQ2673.O69 A2 2016 | DDC 841/.914—dc23
LC record available at http://lccn.loc.gov/2015044423

Contents

Translator's Preface
"Life-Fugues"

Emmanuel Moses was born in Casablanca in 1959, the son of a French-educated German Jew and a French Jew of Polish descent: one an historian of philosophy and the other a painter. He spent his early childhood in France. His parents moved to Israel when he was ten; he lived there until his mid-twenties, and studied history at the Hebrew University of Jerusalem. He then returned to Paris, where he still lives. Prolific, he is the author of twelve collections of poems, as well as a writer of novels, short fiction, and unclassifiable experimental prose. Fluent in four languages, Moses is a translator into French of contemporary Hebrew fiction and poetry, notably of Yehuda Amichai, S. Y. Agnon, and David Grossman; he has edited anthologies of modern Hebrew poetry in translation for the publishers Obsidiane and Gallimard. He also translates from the German and from the English, including poems by C. K. Williams, Raymond Carver, and Gabriel Levin, and some of my own work. Among his other affinities are the French poets André Frénaud, poet of the Résistance, of litanies, of the secret life of words; Franck Venaille, narrator of the local and the working-class quotidian; and the Romanian Jewish German-speaking poet Paul Celan, survivor/refugee who made his own language "other," fragmented and alien.

The poems in this collection come from three recent books: *Préludes et fugues* (2011), *Ce qu'il y a à vivre / What Life Is About* (2012), and *Sombre comme le temps / As Dark as Time* (2014). They show several sides of this versatile, engaging, sometimes enigmatic poet's work: the "Preludes and Fugues" sequence in particular is an ambitious departure from his other books of poems, though rooted in the same preoccupations and knowledge.

The poems from *What Life Is About*, with only numbers as titles, are often quick aperçus, anecdotal, but with a sustained narrative and recurrent themes, even obsessions behind them. Those from *As Dark as Time* add an element of incantation, repetition — there are several virtuoso "list" poems — and dreamlike or hallucinatory encounters.

Throughout his work, Moses' poems often contemplate permanence and vulnerability, focusing on the insubstantiality of what seems at first most solid: a house, a wall, a row of stones. But all the possible, impermanent histories of such structures are implied. A wall can protect or exclude. A house can be abandoned or destroyed. Its inhabitants can be forced out, evicted or deported, with all that that implies both in the history of the Jews in Europe and in the history of Israel and Palestine. An ephemeral-seeming object — a mailbox with a name plate, for example — survives its use and becomes a kind of memorial to the disappeared.

Meditation on history is itself part of a meta-narrative of dialogue, or a longing for dialogue, with the dead. The poet's father, the historian and philosopher Stéphane Moses, remains an interlocutor in his son's work. The elder Moses, one of the second generation of the "Jewish philosophical renewal" exemplified by the writings of Léon Askénazi, André Neher, and Emmanuel Levinas, wrote on 19th and early 20th century European Jewish thought, and the work of Walter Benjamin, Kafka, Celan, Levinas, Gershom Scholem, and Franz Rosenzweig. He died in 2007. The desire for their dialogue to continue, and what seems to remain the paradox of his disappearance, are recurrent strands in the poems:

My father says: I'd like to stop weighing on your shoulders
If you put me down on the ground we could walk side by
    side
I'm not blind or paralyzed
Only a little bit dead
For the moment

Perhaps we could take each other's hands
The way we did when you were little
                    ("Dialogue," *As Dark as Time*)

The poet's mother, the painter Liliane Klapisch, very much alive, is present in the poem "She Painted Artichokes," about a still life she painted (in *As Dark as Time*), and in the poet's own still-life of the painter's work-shoes outside her studio door:

... my mother's old shoes, covered with paint-splashes
Jackson Pollock stains
Came and elbowed me
I had seen them on the floor of her studio
Ageless and childish, a bit like her, after all
....
On the road of life one of them had lost a heel
And the other its shoelace
                    (poem 26, *What Life Is About*)

One might say that the presence of painting and ekphrastic references in the book *Preludes and Fugues* attests to this maternal influence as well.

What Life Is About also attests to, or depicts, with humor and wry self-deprecation, the sexual obsessions of a middle-aged (heterosexual) man, contrapuntal to an individual passion, persistent and troubling, recounted *en filigraine*. None of this would be exceptional, were it not for the novelistic distance the poet takes from his persona, who could sometimes be a character in a novel, more Eastern European or German than French, chain-smoking at his desk or boarding a train, declining his personal preoccupations and fears while the outside world darkens. The poems themselves become enigmatic putative excerpts from a longer narrative that shows the weight of history with a capital H on individual histories — and how those stories (his, hers, yours) in the long run make up the History we are called to remember. This is attested to specifically in a poem that seems to narrate a refusal to participate in an Israeli Defense Force raid on a Palestinian high school, but also, more subtly, in a poem where an urban landscape recalls to the speaker his mother's account of a departure into exile...among other shards in the stained-glass of his narrative. There is unquestionably narrative; there are unquestionably fragments or shards, of which the poet himself has said:

> ...the fragment is something that has been torn off.... It is a displacement and also a dislocation. What is being created thus? A kind of golem, brimming with destructive powers. You still feel the phantom entity from which the scrap has been detached. The result is a text containing pain and a foolish hope for a healing.... The fragment is both the result of a mutilation (of the uninterrupted flow of language) and the hope for a miracle: the restoration of its lost unity.
>
> (Interview conducted by Donna Stonecipher for
> *chicagopostmodernpoetry.com,* 2006)

There is an incantatory or fable-like nature to some of the poems in *As Dark as Time*: litanies of colors, merged identities, multi-generational casts of characters:

> I am the furrier great-grandfather!
> I am the grandfather who prepared smoked fish!
> I am the Prussian grandmother!
> I am the uncle who always gave marvelous gifts!
> I am the great-grandmother, the furrier's widow, the
>   butcher's wife!
>
> ("The Holy Family," *As Dark As Time*)

Dream-scenarios or historical meditations alternate with landscapes peopled with characters always on the point of departure, or traveling towards some feared or desired Elsewhere.

The sequences from *Preludes and Fugues*, which make up the largest part of this collection, make a very different use of "fragmentation," not in the service of an exploded but perceptible single narrative, but in the creation of a text whose structure refers, of course, to music, to Bach's "Well-Tempered Clavier" in particular. The poet chose a theme for each of the cycles, wove information, observation, lyrical or narrative association around and through it, and gave each lyric essay or narrative Prelude a fugal response, an either/or/perhaps to its positing. The "theme" of the first cycle is geographical/historical, a city and its history; the second makes use of myth — Norse and Arthurian; the fourth, of the Book of Ezekiel.

The book was composed with Bach as one of its guiding spirits, and a German landscape as its initial setting. Moses began the sequence after a trip to the city of Speyer, on the Rhine, dominated by its thousand-year-old cathedral, present in Goethe's writings. The view of the cathedral itself, on a hill dominating the city, with flocks of birds circling its dark towers, was what triggered the poet's imagination, and Bach suggested the form. Speyer was also a city where Edith Stein, the Jewish Catholic convert, philosopher and theologian, taught in a Dominican school, before the Nazi regime forbade Jews and those of Jewish origin to teach. Edith Stein was murdered at Auschwitz in 1942; she was beatified in 1987 and sanctified in 1998 — she is the "saint" who bends toward the river in the second Prelude, whom a reader might first have thought was an ekphrastic figure like the red-cheeked girls earlier in the poem:

> I see the shadow of a saint who bends towards the stream
> she is meditating on a passage of Scripture
> the Epistle to the Galatians perhaps or Zacharias
> she is reciting a ballad by Goethe to herself
> each day she stops for a long while between riverbanks
> so the worlds of contemplation and of prayer are separated
> heiress of wise men and merchants
> of peddlers who persist on Rhenish roads in all seasons
> of horse dealers of usurers...
>
> (*Preludes and Fugues*, Cycle A, Prelude 2)

One could say that throughout the series of sequences there is a fugal dialogue — perhaps "fugue" also keeps its other sense of "flight" — between German and Jewish history in Europe, between Christian, pagan and Jewish history over time. The "tree of the world" of the second cycle is a central image of old Norse, thus Germanic, mythology. In the book of Ezekiel, referenced in "Cycle D," it is the ancient Hebrews who are putting cities to the sword, and we seem to see a similar lifegiving tree being destroyed ("Zoan" was the ancient Egyptian capital of the Pharoahs in the second millennium before the Christian era):

> their roots reached down towards abundant waters
> the cedars of God's garden did not equal them
> the cypress could not be compared to their branches
> the plane trees were less than their underbrush
> no tree in God's garden equaled them in beauty
> they were envied by all the trees in God's garden
> their leaf buds multiplied their branches spread
> rage against the fortress fire in the cities
> the day will become darkness
> young men of *No* and *Aven*
> put *Zoan* to the flames
> beneath the great sword of the dead
>
> (*Preludes and Fugues,* Cycle D, Prelude 2)

As well as the preludes and fugues of Bach, the "Todesfugue" / "Death Fugue" of Paul Celan is echoed or enlarged on, and, knowing the poet, I was reminded that Emmanuel Moses' father, to whom so much of his poetry pays homage, was a major critic and interpreter of Celan's work.

Preludes and Fugues in its French edition had no preface and no footnotes: even an erudite reader might have been baffled by the poems' shifting fields of vision and references, or caught up in the shadowed or bright always-shifting landscapes, the multiple stories implied or half-told, figures limned like the saints' tales in quattrocento paintings, moving from frame to frame at the base of the central scene. Most of the sequences are lyrical, but their shape-shifting and multiple frames of reference are modernist. An Anglophone reader might think of Pound or Basil Bunting. As with those poets, however different their pre-occupations, the reader is struck by Moses' polymath and poly-glot sources and themes, by the web of literary, historical and personal references, impossible to unravel, that create a tapestry of European history, Jewish history, myth, mysticism and music.

A polyglot whose experience of the world comes as much from travel and human intercourse as from books, from an in-terrogation of the past which coexists with his experience of the present, Emmanuel Moses is a kind of *Poète sans frontières*. While some contemporary French poets eschew geographical speci-ficity, a perennial subject of Moses' poems is the crossing and the porosity of actual borders, geographical and temporal. A (Proustian?) train of thought set in motion by a pair of old shoes or the light on a building site will move the speaker and the poem itself from Paris to Jerusalem, from a boyhood memory to a 19th-century chronicle, from Bach to Edith Stein. Yet, de-spite his multilingual erudition, the range of his interlocutors, and his obvious pleasure (not in the least doctrinal) in formal ex-perimentation, Moses' poems can also address the reader who engages with his work directly, almost intimately: in turn wry, melancholy, self-deprecating, learned, mercurial, fraternal.

Marilyn Hacker

from *What Life Is About*

1.

If God existed in the darkened synagogue
Or in the church or the cathedral
If he swept the world with his breath
Like the wind tonight announcing winter
Perhaps you'd turn on the lights
Perhaps you'd weatherproof the windows
Perhaps you'd put your hands over your ears
To not hear him pass by

2.

Snow on the rooftops scatters your memories
You didn't think that they'd return so early in the year
Each time these flowers bloom when you least expect it
Spring up from a sound, a light or an odor
From a flock of birds or the strange shape of a cloud
And from so many other marks unrolled with the days' endless
    canvas
The mountain road that led to the house
That you took in the morning going to buy bread
With its rowan tree and the blue distances, white slopes
The warm presence of life there eternally
There was nothing illusory
Nothing untrue

14.

You say "What sins has this immaculate snow come to
    whiten?"
Cars abandoned on the highway give the landscape a look of
    defeat
And I think of the exodus my mother described to me — the
    carts
The cars, horse corpses askew on the pavement
A cigarette between the two of us and we fall in love again
If it burns up, it's to illumine life's glacial night
You've read something somewhere about abandoned children
And their fate
You are an abandoned child, in your own way
Loved but not as you would have wished
Question: Is one ever loved as one would have wished?
With hate, things are always easier
All at once, between the fences and the pallid trees, this
    question
"I wonder if I love detesting you or if I detest loving you?"
    already
Implying its answer
This morning light reverberated on the walls
Like the prolonged vibration of a bell

17.

No one knows where you are right now
Your window looks out over the highway
The Friday evening traffic jams are a potent cry of life
Your parents are laughing, or bored
You don't want any pity
Any fear
Your solitude magnifies you like a peasant's in the midst of his
    field
Or a sailor on the foredeck
Defying the waves
They enter, leave your room discreetly
Doctors, nurses
You're in pain, you don't want to eat or talk
And your sudden ugliness makes you more beautiful
If a sparrow comes to perch behind the windowpane
It's because he knows he has nothing to fear from you
And the crisp sun, the sky with its changing complexion
Are content to set up their scenery there
Like carnies untouched by a city's distress
Who put up their stalls whistling
Because they know that sadness and even death are transient
While joy is eternal

26.

I didn't intend to write about anything
But the cigarette looked for and never found
A sort of legendary cigarette
Like a hoped-for love, Princess Charming
Ravenhair, Snow White or Solveig
But my mother's old shoes, covered with paint-splashes
Jackson Pollock stains
Came and elbowed me
I had seen them on the floor of her studio
Ageless and childish, a bit like her, after all
Gaping, and in that black waiting to be devoured
Something female, and of a woman's sex
That would bewitch men, sons especially
Make them sweat with confusion
On the road of life one of them had lost a heel
And the other its shoelace

38.

"Forgive them…" a drunkard is shoved by youngsters
This evening of blue snow
"Forgive them"
He could be their father, which makes them nastier, more cruel
How beautiful they are, slender, graceful
While he goes squelching through puddles of frozen mud
Like a bear at the end of his chain
"Forgive them" becomes a refrain in the mouth of the splendid
    adolescent
A dark-haired girl with gleaming green eyes
She hums it into his ear
The snowflakes fall on her voice
Making it even sweeter
He ends up spreadeagled, his clumsiness, pushed by one of them
Who would know?
The pure vodka he thought he was sturdy enough to drink like
    water
Has cut his legs from under him, burned his eyes, shrunken his
    heart
To the size of a walnut
Lost in a body still confusing blood and desire

39.

I remember their expressions in the evening when they came back
They had left in the morning, in jeeps and command-cars
In combat uniforms with wooden truncheons at their belts
Orders had been given the previous night in a briefing
To raid a high school and beat up the students
Because they had discovered a cell of the liberation movement in
    the school
I found the commanding officer and told him he could lock me up
But that I wouldn't take part in a lynching
No disciplinary action was taken against me, I spent the day
    reading Dostoevsky
The Brothers Karamazov, though *Crime and Punishment* would have
    been more appropriate
That day there was a chilly winter sun over the mountains
The sky stretched toward the sea where it bent and edged itself
    with fog
Not one of them would open his mouth when they came back
Their faces closed and bitter, their eyes distraught, they undressed
    and went to bed
Without eating, without washing
The silence in the barracks was deafening
I stayed awake, alone, all night, I think
I watched the shadows on the wooden walls
Feeling I had become a shadow myself

40.

A winter day that nothing can exhaust
Because it's gray
And the gray makes bottomless holes in you
Like the naked trees
Like the abandoned factory pierced by the sky
With its raging graffiti that are a declension of despair
A winter day with no imaginable end
Makes you want to sit in some café
And drink the day, drink the winter, drink the unbearable infinite
Within you, outside you

41.

When he meets a young woman he stares into her eyes and most
    of the time
She turns her face away
He remembers having read somewhere that a woman who holds
    a man's gaze is ready to sleep with him
Because it's about that
His will that they all give themselves to him
Those frail, fresh maidens of the city
But what has he to offer them
They see a middle-aged man
Boiling over with desire
Feverish
Go sleep off your black wine of obscene longings
Their very bearing seems to say
Yet sometimes
One of them, out of curiosity or real attraction
Opens the chasm of her pupils wide to him

53.

Tonight I'm nervous
Let the wine flow, even if it's bitter
Let the cigarette burn, even if it scorches my throat
Tonight time chafes and flays me
I think I will sing, even if I lose my voice
I think I will dance, even if I collapse
Tonight I remember you, Father, and a far-off smile
That I don't know if I dreamed or hoped for
I sense the taste of past kisses
I no longer know if they'll last an instant or all night long
Tonight love, tonight death
Make me hallucinate
I think I'll stretch out on my bed, even if my eyes won't close
I think I'll talk to myself in the darkness, even if my lips won't
    move

56.

The time to smoke one more cigarette and you'll fall asleep
The time to write one more letter
In your pocket the keys are heavy as a millstone
Go out and try to walk with a millstone
And the moon will nauseate you
If fear and sorrow didn't take over this way
A musician would change your mood
He'd make you light and gay
But there's no musician anywhere around
Only undertakers and newborns
And boozers and a hothead nicknamed "The Prophet"
Your father wanted to be a prophet too
But it's hard when the mind overrides the guts
You fall asleep and have a long agreeable dream
Be wary of shortening certain lucky moments
The letter will never be mailed
The cigarette is already only a fine gray twig
That will crumble as easily as the dream

59.

Childhood is there, heavy and timorous
He can make it out, moving between thoughts
As he walks from room to room in the house
This morning he got up early
He tried to work and to imagine the encounter
Waiting for him later in the day
Words and desire became mingled
A cup of coffee pushed them both away
And the telephone served as a mailbox
He wanted to turn his back on that child
Who staggered under the wild pepper trees and sycamores
Who hated the pine trees under an inexorable sky
He had trouble breathing
And loving the women around him
Though he thought only of their bodies and of the day's lightness
He didn't sleep at night
The heat was foreign to him
The noises made no sense
Now the marble has become flesh
Light vibrates and bodies hum the melody of endless pleasure
A winter morning sweetens like spring

64.

I'm not afraid of death
I'm not afraid of pain
I'm not afraid of women
I'm afraid
Of course I'm afraid
But I'm not afraid of that fear
Which is like a thick fog inside me
Sometimes it lifts
Sometimes it clears
Sex is one of my religions
And so is a dread so red you'd call it blood
And of one and the other, I'm not afraid, to the point
Of putting my hands over my ears
Of huddling up against an old radiator that barely heats
Of singing to drive the bad things away
My fear is reality reflected in a dream
Or the other way around
I don't know what life is about
I tell you, with great pride, I still don't know

65.

Father, you gave me a beautiful smile the other night
Why don't the dead come in the glare of day?
They come out only at night, like certain animals
And their hunt is finding us
They quench their thirst in the river of our lives
A life where love feeds on memory
How the dead love life!
Sometimes I tell myself that they love it so much it's thanks to
them
That we love it too
And that it loves us in return
I say to myself also that there's no less life on their side than on
ours
You wanted to drink with me in one of those old-fashioned inns
And to walk on the little mountain path where we often talked
And stopped talking to admire the enormous landscape
The clouds, the blue slopes and the gray snow near the peaks
With a lone eagle flying over

70.

"Pisz na Berdyczow!" That means "Write to me at Berdichev!"
Since all the merchants of Poland, Lithuania and Russia
Passed through Berdichev, a main commercial and banking center
of the region
But when commerce moved to Odessa, the city went downhill
quickly
And "Pisz na Berdyczow!" became "Write to nobody!" or "Leave
me alone!"
He writes "Pisz na Berdyczow!" on a piece of paper and tacks it
to his door
But no one reads Polish here, people don't understand what he
meant
So they knock, they ring the bell, they slide messages between the
doorframe and the parquet
They whisper or they shout, they speak rudely or with distinction
According to the circumstances
What can you do under the circumstances?
"Pisz na Berdyczow!"

from *As Dark As Time*

Time in Color

Quick! Colors through the window!
Colors on fields and forests
Before the weather changes
And changes everything
Empties fields and forests of their substance
And ponds and farms
How fleeting the sun is!
How the sky mocks our admiring gaze
Eternity is an optical illusion
Immensity a dubious abstraction
The wheatfields' gold — quick!
The pink of bricks piled on a building-site — quick!
The foliage's chilly green — quick!
The rust-color of bushes, train-tracks, roadbeds, quick!
The yellow of colza in nearly-black fields,
The silver of streams,
The silt-browned green of fish-filled rivers — quick!
Cabbages' purple in well-mannered squares — quick!
The road's grey — quick!
The absolute blue of clear sun-softened autumn days — quick!
Red! Red! Red of tractors, cars, traffic-lights red — quick!
The red of a hunter's cap, his rifle wedged in his armpit — quick!
(And soon the imagined red of a slain beast's blood)
The metallic green of our roadside poplars — quick!
Blue slate roofs — quick!
The blue of distant mountains — quick!
Stone blue, horizon blue,
Blue light falling in a fine mist on the world — quick!
And white — I had almost forgotten white — the white of dusty
    roads,
The white of cows lazing in pastures — quick!
Omnipresent white, that the eye disdains

Of a wall between two cypresses, of trucks going swiftly past
White — quick!
Then black! Black! The black of fertile earth ploughed over and
    over again — quick!
The black of a horse driven mad by the trains
Who gallops in crazed circles alongside the fence — quick!
The black of a village chimney silent as a closed mouth — quick!
The black of a village church-bell never to be caught up in the
    savior's arms — quick!
White, black, green, pink, blue and gold —
Quick! Quick! Quick!

Dialogue

My father says: I'd like to stop weighing on your shoulders
If you put me down on the ground we could walk side by side
I'm not blind or paralyzed
Only a little bit dead
For the moment
Perhaps we could take each other's hands
The way we did when you were little
Now I'm the one who's little
But I'll grow
I have all eternity for that.
I say to my father:
One day, you know, you'll be so light
That I'll start to run
Along the road and across the fields
I'll leap so high they'll think I'm a stag
Clever indeed the one who can catch me
Till then I'll stoop
I'll bend
Under your weight that crushes me like the sky
And the nebulous weight of the stars

Prayer

God of drizzle and resonant earth
Give us the strength to get through bad days
God of exotic birds and astounding flowers
Give us the joy of the sun streaming through a tangle of branches
God of sap and fog
Give us the sensual sweetness, the melancholy sweetness
Of the seasons passing

A House and a Wall

In front of this foundation, its rows of perbend stones thrusting
    up from the ground
Where grass still grows
In front of this germ of private life
In front of this absence already reeking of abandonment
How not to stop
Not muse and reflect
On what is after all
Like a strange entombment

"A wall always has two sides," said the worker
"A wall always has two sides," said the poet
"A wall only has one side," said the soldier
"A wall only has one side," said the politician
"A wall only has one side," said the villager
"Walls don't exist," said the prisoner
"Walls don't exist," said the child
"Walls don't exist" said the lovers

A house is born from no earth
No sky or stars
No trees
A house, one day, will be everything
You'll move in, you'll leave it
You'll be evicted, expelled, it will be illegally occupied
It will be paradise and hell
An ideal attained, a nightmare come to life

"I don't have time to die," says the living man
"I don't have time for resurrection," says the dead man
From the two sides of the wall
Two sides of the bones

The poet says "I saw that in my childhood — a house swallowed up
In the dark of night."
The dead man lights a cigarette — why not?
The living man coughs and spits on the mud that will be a floor or a wall
The dead man blows on his finger-bones laughing
The living man doesn't want to think about the plot of land before his eyes any more
The cigarette goes back and forth from the dead to the living, from the living to the dead
The poet will never climb the wall
Will never build a house
But he will eat up his life in cigarettes, love, dreams
Sick with time

Your Shadow

That night I dreamed of a novel whose title was your name
Someone had thrown it away in the street with other books
The writer's name was the same as yours too
Are you here or somewhere else?
Do you walk in the streets all day long
The way you did with me beside the gray river?
What do you think of when you close your eyes, just as you fall
    asleep?
We don't see each other anymore, or speak to each other
I wonder how you arrange your hours
What you do with words and images
The ones you keep, the ones you throw away, as I do
If you live the present moment like a bridge suspended above
    an abyss
That the slightest weight, the slightest breath, could wash away
Or like a territory vast as the tundra
With no before and no after
You have gone away taking your sorrow
But you forgot a scrap of your shadow at the door

My Father, Me, and Everything Else

You'd say it was my father but it's me
You'd say it was the sun but it's the moon
You'd say it was a bird but it's an airplane
You'd say it was the sky but it's the sea
You'd say those are stars but they're satellites
You'd say it was a forest but it's a cemetery
You'd say it was a prayer but it's a declaration of love
You'd say it was a declaration of love but it's a declaration of war
You'd say it was his daughter but it's his wife
You'd say it was his wife but it's his daughter
You'd say it was a man but it's a woman
You'd say it was gold but it's iron
You'd say it's fireworks but it's a bombardment
You'd say it was laughter but it's tears
You'd say he was alive but he's dead
You'd say he was dead but he's quite alive
You'd say it was a landscape but it's an interior
You'd say it was a dream but it's reality
You'd say he was a madman but it's the others who are mad
You'd say it was evening but it's high noon
You'd say it was a pool of water far off but it's a mirage
You'd say it was a curse but it's a blessing
You'd say it was a memory but it's a prediction
You'd say it was a repetition but it's the first time
You'd say it was music but it's a creaking door
You'd say it was an eye but it's a cloud
You'd say it was a cloud but it's a swan
You'd say it was simple but it's complicated
You'd say it was a tear but it's a pearl
You'd say it was a sword but it's a laser beam
You'd say it was a sleeping city but it's a city awakening
You'd say it was a hospital but it's a detention center

You'd say it was a secret but it's an official announcement
You'd say it was a bar but it's a temple
You'd say it was you but it's your sister
You'd say it was me but it's my son
You'd say it was space but it's the inside of a tin can
You'd say it was cloth but it's skin
You'd say it was the hereafter but it's the here-and-now
You'd say it was a demon but it's an angel
You'd say it was a child but it's an adult
You'd say it was a rainbow fallen to earth but it's a splotch of oil
You'd say it was ink but it's water
You'd say it was wine but it's ink
You'd say it was courage but it's fear
You'd say it was the beginning but it's the end
You'd say it was the end but it's the beginning

Meditation

For Marcel Cohen

What happens to the mailboxes of demolished houses?
What do they do to perform their task whatever happens?
Because mail can continue to arrive
Sometimes even decades after it was posted
— I received a postcard today that my father wrote thirty-four
    years ago
With a picture of a nineteenth-century advertisement
"Waiter! An Inca Cola!" —
Sometimes they remain attached to a wall that holds up nothing
    but emptiness
That separates one emptiness from another
They age slowly
Rust, gape open, distorted like age-tormented faces
Always bravely displaying
The names of long-dead residents
Eternal addressees in brass or copper card-holders
Often the address has disappeared
If not the whole street, replaced by a newer, wider one
Or by a playground, a mall, a parking lot
But they continue to sport an air of being at the center of the
    world
And they're not altogether wrong in that
For nothingness is the secret heart of being
Brushing off the nonsense of the situation with a stoic's or a
    cynic's haughtiness
They contemplate the person passing by
Whom they invite to meditate on permanence and
    impermanence
The visible and the invisible
Time and space

Memory and forgetfulness
The one who tears them from their supports
To use them as decorations or sell them to the ironmonger
To throw them on the closest dump or keep them as souvenirs
Is like someone who uproots a strong-rooted tree
He digs a hole that never will be filled
He kills the dead a second time
While their voices cry out from the depths.

A Stolen Dream

In my dream I asked to speak
I went up to the platform
I gave someone else's speech
The men and the women in the audience
Were divided by an aisle
As they would be in a synagogue
While reciting the stolen speech
I realized that the dream wasn't mine either
I was in someone else's dream
As I might be in the body of someone else's wife
I thought that this other person might be dead
And that he had willed me his dream
Or that perhaps I had killed him
To steal his dream from him
I thought that perhaps I myself was dead
And that I was dreaming a living man's dream
In order to linger in life a little longer
The way vampires nourish themselves with fresh blood
So as not to die entirely
And the speech
Was in fact about death, or about the dead, more precisely
And about the continual birth of those who survive them
But as I continued my remarks
I was thinking that, on the contrary, faced with the dead,
    survivors die too
They die tirelessly
At every moment of their miserable existence
I said "There is light,"
And I was thinking "There is no light."
It seemed as if dead leaves were coming out of my mouth
That they emerged in continuous waves and fell silently all
    around me

It seemed as if they were falling on the silent audience
That was not made up of living beings after all
But of shop window dummies
Male and female
White, so blinding white under the dead leaves
That arose from within me and perhaps came from all the
cemeteries

Stones

Revere a wall and it becomes venerable
There are those who refuse to understand that
I'm not defending idolatry
But thoughts and prayers transform the things they address
Incantations changed the giant stones called megaliths
Dolmens, menhirs, cairns
Aligned as at Stonehenge
No cave would be sacred without someone seeking
    transcendence
I'd discuss this with my father
We'd drink coffee, he'd be lying down or propped up in an
    armchair
I was always nervous
I had to prove something
Now I find him everywhere
Death bestows omnipresence
In death time is at last reversible
The field where galgals are lined up as far as the eye can see
    becomes my father's ghost
Am I the Prince of Denmark for all that?
I don't need a watchtower or a night patrol
Or black midnight
Sometimes I'd talk nonsense
The coffee was never strong enough
I dived into a whirlpool of dead men
Wholeheartedly
Wasting my time
And beyond the windowpane the sky was breathing
Insensible to our fates
Which was why I loved it
As a man might love a woman for her indifference

She Painted Artichokes

For my mother

You had nothing to say so you painted some splendid artichokes
You took them from the kitchen and placed them on a black
    chair
You didn't think about it
You had no doubts
You went from the kitchen to the studio
Like a priest passing from the sacristy to the altar
The all had turned to nothing
And now this nothing became something once again
The artichokes told the extraordinary story of green
And the chair the humble tale of black
Their stories were like those told by old women
On the village square, near the fountain
At the close of day
Filaments of time, of life
That are no longer anything and once were everything
And become something again in the tender evening light
You had nothing to say, so you took your brushes and palette
    knife
You pressed the tubes of paint
And you painted metaphysical vegetables
On an existential chair
You told the extraordinary tale of everything turned to nothing
Re-transformed into something by a pair of artichokes

My Life

Mother, I'm taking my life with me
Father, I'm taking my life with me
Woman, you are taking my love, I see you on the dusty road
Where once we kissed

Let the sun dance on women's backs
Let the rain hammer men's hands
Let life drown itself in fumes of wine
Let death flee like a pickpocket

Mother, you hide your tears under the pillow
Like a miser hiding gold coins
Father, you hide your face under the earth
And your feet are planted in the clouds

Woman, I carry my shame in the depths of my pockets
I drink and I smoke what doesn't fit there
One day I will be Cain
I'll be pursued for what I did with my life

My arms will never embrace the sun
My mouth will never drink up all the rain
Life will go to the devil
I'll catch up with old death

Father, it's time to sleep
Mother, it's time to leave
Woman, dust can be a lovers' bed
Shame weighs down my steps on every road

The Holy Family

I am the furrier great-grandfather!
I am the grandfather who prepared smoked fish!
I am the Prussian grandmother!
I am the uncle who always gave marvelous gifts!
I am the great-grandmother, the furrier's widow, the butcher's wife!
I am the bookseller great-grandfather!
I am the angry uncle!
I am the sad cousin!
I am the aunt broken by the loss of her daughter!
I am the Polish grandmother!
I am the grandfather hero of the First World War!
I am the shoemaker great-grandfather!
I am the doctor ancestor!
I am the trapper ancestor!
I am the ancestor who sold cooking oil!
I am the alcoholic aunt!
I am the athletic uncle!
I am the cousin who was lost — and found — on the mountain!
I am the crazy great-aunt!
I am the secret agent great-cousin!
I am the sex-crazed great-uncle!
I am the great-grandmother always in a hurry, always arriving
     early!
They take their turns entering and exiting
Everyone in the lobby of the inn is drunk
Each time the door opens
An icy draft sweeps in
Carrying a few snowflakes
Who is paying the actors?
A traveler who arrived the previous day
The players are students, vagabonds, pensioners
Who go along with the farce for booze and a hot meal.
When someone asks the man the title of his show
He answers "The Holy Family."

Portrait of My Friend

He had been waiting for me for five years
Behind drawn venetian blinds
We talked right away about hatchets and revolvers
The frozen sea, the whole caboodle
He no longer wrote a word
He saw nobody
Because literature had lost all interest for him
Since you earned less with it than by selling tomatoes
And because his friends were now
Black inscriptions on white stones
Tormenting his persistent memories
He had had enough of the noise of the city
The noise of the family
The noise of the past
He hoped for a silent future
Saw himself in beloved cities, their streets deserted
Through motionless nights
In the arms of taciturn and tender women
A river would flow
Discreet as everything outsize
You could make out the wind only from the contortions of flags
And leaves rustling
On the trees of refined gardens
And still later there would be nothing but nothing
This thought transformed his face into a smile
His eyes into suns
The tobacco in the bowl of his pipe glowed too
Dark as time
Burning like life

Preludes and Fugues

Cycle A

Impassable threshold — I was amidst the roses
the old bridge's parapet astride the stream
had served me often as a pew
that evening I understood at last that I ought not enter
the nave of the past
nor that of the soul
drunkenness of one who has no more words
for whom language becomes tongue and speech
I no longer fear the intruder
o my hostile brother
Esau
one day I will catch up with you, my heavy steps
weighed down with milky bleeding life
o prior creature
this evening I sated myself on your crimson
as you once did on mine
still steaming the spiced wine quenched our thirst
at the moment of our bargain
and I think I remember that we sang
one of us wept from stupid joy or from excess feeling
none of this was very elegant
outside a lame man asked our father's
gardener for alms
impassable threshold
I was amidst the ashes

Fugue I

The hawks are still circling the turrets
they circle backwards in time
the sky is gray and the cathedral looks like the pink
bloody mass
of a flayed animal
tall trees bristle at its feet
offering it their venerable boughs
the leaves that rustle at a storm's approach...
threshold uncrossed as if forbidden
silence of narrow streets of buildings with closed shutters
at the feet of the huge carcass
whose stripped flesh is a prayer to the living God
mumbled by a millennium of mouths
murmuring in the silence of nightfall
the multitudes of sleeping mouths
as many as those of the day's pilgrims
or even more
circling and rising to battle the gray sky
where the proud birds' paths cross
grief beats against the hillsides
it swells as dusk progresses
heat and the first raindrops
vibrate with the bells
sad and yellow as the light is too
as an invalid's face glimpsed behind a window
framed by lace curtains' angel wings
impassable threshold — of the soul's vast vessel

PRELUDE 2

O you cut down from the gallows
o ashes around the stake
I see venerable family men beneath the bloody banner
how heavy is Germany's silence!
Leaning on an ash tree a child looks at me
he has his own appointments which he will keep later
The girls astride the bridge's parapet hum songs
they don't even glance at the stream deceiving them
heiresses of red-cheeked craftsmen, their own joys
and numerous sorrows flow through their veins
how silence weighs beneath straying clouds
I see the shadow of a saint who bends towards the stream
she is meditating on a passage of Scripture
the Epistle to the Galatians perhaps or Zacharias
she is reciting a ballad by Goethe to herself
each day she stops for a long while between riverbanks
so the worlds of contemplation and of prayer are separated
heiress of wise men and merchants
of peddlers who persist on Rhenish roads in all seasons
of horse dealers of usurers
of so many exiles
o hanged men the gallows' flowers in all seasons
family men beneath the fiery banner
how the past weighs on our shoulders adult and child
how our names weigh
among the willows and ash trees
between the current and the cathedral's enormous dream

FUGUE 2

Where was the truth and where the lie?
Did what might have been exist somewhere?
In the long chain of transfigurations it wasn't impossible
that one evening in the Palatinate nature held its breath
cities followed one after another towns and villages
such tranquility offered to the traveler!
In orchards trees bent under the weight they bore
I saw swallows
bandits, conscripts, escaped prisoners
so many stories raised with the dust
on roads which time had failed to erase
one sitting on the edge of a well saw the Savior appear
perhaps he taught him a thing or two
from that day on he prowled the forest and spoke with wild
    beasts
where is the truth and where the lie?
Who built the church where the whole world huddles?
Flowers arose like praise around it
hollyhocks and campanula
nature held its breath for the hidden ceremony
which would be pierced only by the pearly brooch of a bunch
    of asparagus
fifty-two angels kept watch from portal to chevet
vespers had been rung and love...
in a dim tavern gypsy fate hung on a throw of the dice
history prowled from pillage to pillage
on roads which time had not erased

PRELUDE 3

No one needs to answer to eternity
not beings — lovers or birds
nor things
nor even the elements linked in dark conspiracy
No need to have stopped just there
and set down time's suitcase
salvation will not come from anywhere
but the passage of hours counted like rosary beads
at the cathedral's base so many shadows flutter
mortals waiting or wandering
they were the ones you followed down narrow lanes
transfixed by desire
they were carrying time's suitcase
what law impelled them forward and circling
if not the endless cycle of the seasons?
Finally they broke the spell
perhaps they'll lead their gangs again between the Rhine and
    the Moselle
saviors of sacks and string
swallows swirled with hawks at the yellow edge of the storm
they sketched your fate

FUGUE 3

The ancient prayer stayed beside the door
like a welcoming host looking out for travelers to invite into his
    residence
stone dominates iron
but it is all matter!
What I inherited defies space defies time
death has not triumphed
it is all matter!
I loved you from avatar to avatar
and now I swallow dust's potion in long drafts
to mix you with my black blood
you accompanied the lovers to the threshold
impassable threshold
you stayed at the door like a vigilant guard
so that they could become one
you were not of this world either
while it breathed into the lovers' breath
and ran in their black blood
all is matter!
Even the passing sounds of music
and the shadows of the living like those of the dead
leaned that evening over water where a black swan drifted
I was looking less for my own face's reflection
than for a thought's, an image from a dream
I saw a familiar cohort
                       a shadow patrol

PRELUDE 4

We were obliged to come into the world
here as elsewhere
like the ass reluctant to leave the stable
since thistles seem small recompense for hay
he refuses to come forward brays for darkness
for silence enclosed in the boards of his stall
Who plays the thankless role of master?
Who kicks against what authority?
We did not ask to be born
to cross the first threshold
impassable threshold
we arrived and were of this world
while wanting nothing to do with this world
hospitable smiles masked the unacceptable
dug deeper daily
the shadow thickened by the roadside
caressing the couch-grass and brambles
poppies brought back the first abandonment
those poignant evenings
we would not go forward we claimed the lost part
in a silence of closed lips
we didn't want a love already pushing us away

FUGUE 4

The moment of coincidence arrives
is it the moment of grace?
Was it the moment of grace?
As we might speak of a stroke of good luck
evoked one evening in the lindens' shadow
in a quiet little square
a coincidence of heart and absence
otherwise called desire and mourning
that evening first one and then the other
one reflected in dirty water before the other
and what is this dirty water but our look our memory then we
    turn away
the moment of capture arrives
is there grace in capture?
I remember a passage toward live limpid water
rays veered with the current they turned back
I watched them as I waited for what was strange
was that the moment of grace?
The evening poured out separation
who had said in the lindens' shadow that he had come closer to
    truth?
to the essence which is what is strange
                     his own wanderings
a laugh filled a room's golden cube
that memory would expand, one evening in a quiet square
to an eye that would reach the firmament

Cycle B

Knight of the deep wound
I see that there is an ash tree…
when the universe has foundered
I will find shelter there
I, son of one of the virgins
I know that there is a tree
the first one to lose its leaves
they call it the tree of the world
its roots are sunk deep into ice
the tips of its branches decked with mist
I will find shelter there
with the other men of the middle world
with the leaves trembling on the heavenly path
they say that it is watered by a fountain of tears
that Hecuba and Andromache could once be seen there
                                  proud women's shadows
but also Achilles and David mourning their companions
I know that there is an ash tree called the tree of the world
it rises under the dew
moaning
I will find shelter there
beneath the sun's wings and the millstone of black clouds
there is a tree of the world
o people of the middle world

FUGUE 1

We are all those trees of which I said:
                        I know there is a tree
we embrace three worlds
                           we are the tree of the world
the living and the dead touch in us
              the dead rise toward the living
              the living descend toward the dead
we are the middle
        o world of men
which is the world of the gods
            the mortals rise toward the immortals
            the immortals descend toward the mortals
who lives at the top of the ash tree if not the most joyous of the
    gods?
Or perhaps it was wind in the boughs?
In us the dead rise toward the immortals
the immortals lean down toward the dwelling place of the dead
if the ash tree is green before the oak
if the oak is green before the ash
we will or will not watch raindrops on the windowpane
blur the view it offers of the sky
we are the tree of the world
            the dead nourish the gods
            the gods grow with the living
I know that there is a tree

PRELUDE 2

The sun was their gold
who remembers that they took so long to start again?
Dogs and doves sought the branches' shadow
but no serpent ever lingered there
someone had fled to Norway on a cutter
a woman pregnant by a foreigner
she passed there amidst the saplings
that sheltered her in their leaves
when they had set sail
she shed tears for her father, her brothers and handmaidens
once out of the forest she never returned
who would have told her where the tree of the world could be
    found?
But she had seen the great vegetal procession!
Later she would often pick up her lute
and sing of sylvan beauty
where in summer she had sought cool and calm
where the sun was her gold
old betrayals smoldering like brushfire…
in a castle in Norway
a woman would pick up her lute
and call on the tree of the world

Fugue 2

Or perhaps she died
as the wives of fallen soldiers sometimes do
her son will take the saddest name
and will become a hero in his turn
sung by poets from court to court
or perhaps she took up her lute to intone a lament
between the walls of her nun's cell
or she could have woven a tapestry for her beloved
which shows two armies before their confrontation
knights in armor with painted shields and plumed helmets
foot soldiers armed with halberds banners
and in the background bouquets of trees at the foot of blue hills
one of them spiked with a pink fortress
where she would imagine herself seated at the window
fearfully waiting
for the outcome of the fray
a chaffinch would be perched on the branch of a walnut tree
that defines the world
and builds it
it could be said the tree kept it balanced
recognizable from far off and always solitary
the woman would pass long hours depicting it in the landscape
tree-world with packets of dry leaves
hanging over it a sun sending out long rays
which will be their gold

PRELUDE 3

I will sing in bird language
or like the organs of Dresden
there was an old woman who still remembered them
beneath the syringas of exile
(and now she sleeps in a sad suburban cemetery)
a linden used to shade her grave but I'm told it was cut down
words of smoke will emerge from my mouth
when I sing in the tongue of the bird of paradise!
They'll have called me guilty, a vagabond
till I raise my song toward the evening's blue clouds
how strong the wind is at nightfall
it unfurls flags of smoke between the gallows
each one was the tree of knowledge
lit by a guilty sun
I will sing between brick walls
dragging my vagabond feet from hut to hut
each rag drying in the wind will be a shroud for me
we drank down great mouthfuls of gall!
There were days when the wind exulted
even the sun was guilty —
o vagabonds huddled in ditches in vacant lots
o sleepers in eternity's hot morning
two by two the shadows withdraw toward the bend in the road
the world's marvels will have to step aside
with the streaming light

FUGUE 3

Here rose a bravely woven song
— the assassin's whistling in back alleys —
bread that was delivered gnawed by rats
or at any rate spotted with mold
o unscrupulous bakers of the dismal years!
Mothers you kept your little girls close by your skirts
— the ogres whistling in back alleys —
mornings were pale and hard as bone
life rotted in foul-smelling kitchens
no one drank wine in leafy bowers
at most a beer or two between factory walls
we lived in city centers under the purr of machines
sirens ripped the morning fog
sometimes we thought we were on the road to the sun!
Men and women had exchanged their roles
they drowned the wound as best they could
sailors left on the dock sang with peasants beneath the earth
they died beside the factory
without sacraments
cursing those who cursed them and kicked them aside
now we can see the oblivion where an insane chimney grows
what became of the songs and wisps of smoke?
Which god spared the last tree in the world?

PRELUDE 4

To be this in oneself — and outside oneself
to liquefy to grow
given over to the care of an internal chemistry
to stand for a day in solitary beauty
within oneself outside oneself in the midst of a field
or, yes, on the slope sketched by the same light
at that vague hour which is arrival and departure
flux reflux impoverishment wealth
an over-profusion even of absence!
When an invisible bell sounds for meditation
or a flock of birds traces a moving border
between two spaces two shapes two regimes
at that hour only the tree sings its own pure spirit
it becomes a hymn itself
its freedom rises like a plume of smoke
pure and magnificent
perpetual transformation at one's core
fed by the same water the same light
as those streaming outside
for the tree within is the tree
as a word vibrates when thought
as speaking of a woman loved and lost brings her back
lightly touching the books as she crosses the bedroom
bent fleetingly over your right or your left shoulder

FUGUE 4

Light at day's end — to be that
a fawn and green condensation
the desolate point facing which ocean
direct like an opening
and as vertiginous
green childhood light at the peninsula's tip
point at the edge point at the end of the honed day
precious light
that a lighthouse beam evoked in the night
but changed
revealed
salvation come from elsewhere across so many veils
so many shadows murmurs so much stone
who would notice it through the length of the day?
Evening brought to the simple garden
choice and metamorphosis
its upright honesty slashed through space
where somewhere beyond the cypresses a fountain splashed…

Cycle D

It will be emptied bit by bit
but fire won't cleanse that mass of rust!
I put my blood on the naked rock
there was no blood left on the wood scraps
let the sword smite —
it is the great sword of the dead
they let out a war cry
they lay out rams for sacrifice
before the great trembling
you collapse and you were a splendid heifer
you did not have time to pack your bags
iron-fed soldier whose rust won't be scraped off
scraps of all wood
more blood on the scrap-heap
bronze scrap on the woodpile before the collapse
misfortune be damned
I also have spoken
and eaten the rust bit by bit
go gather up the pieces still there
by the door — bloodthirsty!

FUGUE 1

Great sword of the dead…
the wind from the East broke you
on the sea's breast
your seamen and sailors
and all the men of war and all the passengers
will flow in the sea's heart
cane and reeds
gold and wool
flowed with you
the wind made you shiver
as you did at the hour of the fall
— the birds can no longer be heard
if a word crumbles away
it leaves a hole as its sole trace
quickly abandoned
there will be no more traces the windy day roars
who will remember the sensuality of shadows
Gone now from the seas
the wind makes islands shiver on the horizon
at the hour of the fall
taken onto the high seas
the wind broke you
you declared "I am with God"
to your murderers' faces
you made yourself into a heart like the heart of God

PRELUDE 2

Justice of the *No* — the multitude of *No* — the line is breached
    at *Aven* —
the waters spill out among the clouds
rage against *Sin*
for the waters have increased the abyss have enlarged it
because of the abundant waters that made it grow
— it was beautiful in its greatness
the one and the other like trees
higher than all the trees in the countryside
in their branches nested all the birds of the air
in their shade were seated a great number of people —
they were beautiful in their greatness
                        and their spread branches
their roots reached down towards abundant waters
the cedars of God's garden did not equal them
the cypress could not be compared to their branches
the plane trees were less than their underbrush
no tree in God's garden equaled them in beauty
they were envied by all the trees in God's garden
their leaf buds multiplied their branches spread
rage against the fortress fire in the cities
the day will become darkness
young men of *No* and *Aven*
put *Zoan* to the flames
beneath the great sword of the dead

FUGUE 2

With those who went down....
they went down
with the daughters of nations
                    with all the multitude
went down
                    with their tombs
                    with the uncircumcised
                              among the victims of the sword
multitude victim of the great sword
within the sight of all that multitude
when I spread my net
how it troubled the waters
amidst the luminous foam!

PRELUDE 3

It was winter: our hearts darkened once more
no fog that didn't hide the truth from these and those
wolves raised their bitter cry
and the moon had frozen in the ponds…
when one of the strayed ewes was found
our hearts clenched
                              without sheepfolds
so often reduced to darkness
gripped by the cold
who remembered shepherds?
Even the sky seemed to have forgotten them
but if a flock of swans flew by
exhaled like a perfume from its blue arch
we drew back our shoulders
it was still winter
frost spread its desolate glare
often our hours of walking
pasture after pasture
gave nothing but a huge slashed hope
the lookout could see no longer
and the one who had stationed him there
hid according to the season's nature

FUGUE 3

In his homilies on Ezekiel, Gregory the Great wrote
that holy books sometimes indicate the time sometimes the place
to point to truths they don't state outright
divine eloquia aliquando ex tempore aliquando ex loco
causas designant quas aperto semone non indicant
Hiemes erat: it was winter
thus the heart's cold is revealed (*frigus cordis*)
far from pillars vaults cloisters porches galleries
there where adoration is replaced
by simple childlike pleasures
it was also winter
one past melted into another
despite all distances
the beasts' steaming breath and the white light
kept two dirigibles attached
as they crossed the sky at the wind's whim
laughter replaced swearing come from the same snow

PRELUDE 4

Go out onto the plain where many a traveler raised his head
at the cawing of cranes as they flew by
how can you in this life — you will ask yourself —
undo the bonds of mortality?
You will think "I am in chains"
above you clouds will trace white paths
amidst the azure
no companion will cross your path
and yet this plain is wide as the world!
The birds of the sky will have cast their shadow on the roads of
    the world
here many and many a traveler raised his head
before going on between the squares of wheat of earth of snow
solitary shadow beneath a glaring cloudbank
mute shadow
how to cut death's knots
in this vast world
which is like a plain where you hear yourself called
even by a moaning
        a cawing in the clouds
shadow — flame — shadow
arise and go forth
perhaps I will speak to you
and I arose and went out on the plain...

FUGUE 4

Some came from far off
well beyond the plains
they have knights' bold deeds on the tip of their tongues
you hear them beneath an inn's blackened timbers
you forget the nagging question
born on the road
from the wheatfields to the forest
you listen to them…
a child once again at the foot of the table
who stretches his neck to miss not a word of the story
who raises his head
like many a traveler at the cranes' cry
the meat got cold on the platter
but with your heart aflame
you imagined yourself a hero beyond the plain…

Cycle E

Here nature weeps and moans
we don't know why
which makes it seem more dreadful
are those death-rattles mixed with sobs of revolt
of mourning?
Trees wind ocean — all of them emit a piercing cry
but this music with its deep organ tones
is as strange and mysterious as a hymn
an enormous psalm
for those swallowed up by masses of water or clods of earth
for nature united in its single nameless
                                    martyrdom
the bramble with the crab
the sailor and the stone
darkness meets the wailing
at night! Night! Night...
whirlpools smoke fog
a funeral procession goes wild in monstrous forms
the incredible breathes and freezes
perhaps this is a dream of alarm and knell
of assassinations and ghosts
a dream of damnation
where light itself is a witness for the prosecution
death is at the keyboard — epidemic!

FUGUE 1

He is sad in the evening and sad in the morning
the crow mocks Narcissus!
A winter landscape lies down and then rises inside him
without the childish joy it used to give
humiliation of each heavy step
the shivering makes him cry
I would like — he thinks — to understand better than the ox
and not be content to assuage my hunger on hedges like the ram
growing old is the final wound
with illness — lurking at the core of bodies
trembling there beneath a ray of light
from a sky where rain's wasted hours flow away
gray hours
like a leaf buried in the bed
soon dry and creased
soiling the bed
and what's this madness
a revolt against the universe —
no human heart has ever spoiled the feast
with its meager spattering
circular landscape where his fate turns round
dark with all its secrets
dim subject of a night with one partisan
that he bangs against
the insult his sun flung at the sun —

PRELUDE 2

They go down and come up again:
hell of urinals, hell of the métro!
Real life is subterranean
those who believe in dreams prefer not to wake
those who insist on god stroll from dawn till dusk in the nave
cradled by the perfume of confessions
the city throbs with death and resurrection
beneath the rusty gaze of weathervanes
you find the moon where you can
they carry it away in their possession
the devil undresses you with his imps
but the angelic cohort leaves no soul naked
for the soul is the body
the city dupes the bodies which had dreamed
that they were hoisting the white flag at last
that they would be given the sky and the clouds
that their eyelids would glisten with golden sand
you're ashamed so you whistle
because you're in the cauldron
and your fingers are filthy
they dream at the wrong time
they get up at the wrong time
sometimes the hospital vanquishes the summer
there are harmonies that grip your throat
sublimities

FUGUE 2

Penitence!
Thus the angels' perfume
pervades the streets
the multitudes
you'd say an aerial dance
with the prayers of every solitary heart
sometimes one of them says — I've bloomed **again**
and then his soul enfolds his body
as the city's soul enfolds the streets
or time the clock-towers in the squares
sometimes one of them says: the time I enfold **has stopped**
it has departed
for time is the body
as night encloses the gaze
which is its brightness
or its heart
the moon was night's proud heart
a spirit on time's tightrope
who mocks himself
for being mute and yellow
underground needles have stopped time
they mount and descend
more trapeze artists!
Above the multitudes

PRELUDE 3

Depths which are not only shipwreck
You haven't slid down to them!
All this classicism will float up
in stiff tufts
not one will veer away
from the epicenter
the merman had a bass voice
he would sing like a street musician
from the depths of the abyss
that fierce fairground —
toward which shore of the abyss?
Here are sounds that will pierce the waves' skin
in the name of the classical
                              past
ropes of algae
you stop moving
rhyming with nothing
is not word-play
shipwreck deep in the epicenter
                    that
is the storm nothing will bifurcate
threads of umber and amber gushing
through the water's translucent skin
seen from the depths of the night

FUGUE 3

Planks simply there
                    set far apart, but what does it matter
what does it matter   where
useless   gushing they lean
at an undefined angle
secret secret
          they move aside
in tufts stiff as rods
rigid   oh my despairing one
so much kelp with no nave
             no deck from now on
lost planks
caressed   menaced
     cadaverized
by the sea
stiff crossings-out
        of bones
               with no country or ancestry
illusion! Madness!
Under the eye of the demon who can't unclench his hand
with all the comings and goings
between the previous abyss
        and the abyss that came after
you were a spoiled child in paradise
then prince of a false kingdom

PRELUDE 4

The bulldozed road follows a valley's meanderings
we are in the Balkans or some suburb, what do I know
maybe Central America, let's say Mexico
everyone drives too fast, everyone works hard to live
but their hearts are generous as the volcanoes spilling lava
blood seeks only to rejoin blood
you'll be taken where you want to go
and if there are no seats left, what's the difference
you'll hang on to the outside door
standing on the running-board gripping a fender, if you have the
     guts
you'll surely get where you're going
the road's wretched state is because
of the civil war or the endemic corruption that nips
any development project in the bud
the passengers show their good humor by singing folksongs
about love solitude and ghosts
"I used to work on the railway" says the driver, sticking his head
     out of the bus
dogs in front of the farmers' houses bark
at the bus as it races by
yet the countryside doesn't exist except as a memory
you don't know where you're really going :
down, always further down toward the red earth.

FUGUE 4

O forest of earth and fog!
Everything was razed, and the old houses wander
ghosts in their own right above empty lots
the city is nothing now

                since unemployment but really since the war
if only water had claimed its rights —
yet it's not very distant
it hurls dreams at the docks
each pile vibrates like a violin string at its shivering touch
"We were magnificent" say ancient voices,
          voices of trade
fog that once embellished their ships
softens the contours of hovels

               and demolitions
o sooty earth billows of brick and planks that the rain has polished
poverty — dreadful — is a precious metal
Who still comes dancing to a lovers' rendezvous beside the bicycle
    shop?
No trembling hand now scrawls a woman's name on the last walls
get up, fog
bring forth from the shadows and silence
dockers' ghosts above the piers
a man in black meets his past
he has the elegance of an old-fashioned suitor
he moves slowly away on the potholed asphalt
between vacant lots where magic is still gliding —

Cycle G

It was already evening in the west
veiled with the heart's tawniness after a dark day
when tears were drying
losing their transparency bit by bit
to take on the opacity of sadness
the water keeps its mirror brightness
beneath the gaudy sunset
as if a prophet had painted his lamentation on the sky
he too knew the sorrows of the fleeing lover
it will all redden later
the cloak and the sleeping man
like a yearly holiday
but without oysters or bells
instead of the body the potion made fruitful
a meadow will burst into flower in spring
to give fresh grief back to life
the sunset murmuring in the landscape
love was that blue that tender yellow resisting fate
and order made fruitful by what opposes it
among the seagulls the hesitant hour veiled its tears
the fleeing sun betrayed the golden vase

FUGUE 1

Burning Ophelia! There is a god
turned to marble like all the dead
where are the gawkers where are the mockers
and the representatives of earthly powers?
A corpse composes the landscape in the shadow of a barrel-hoop
still burning
still a body that weighs on the earth
thus the water gives way beneath the weight of the eternal fiancée
                                        garlanded with flowers
thus the countryside proclaims its mourning
vesperal ruins shaded by branches where the melancholy of a
      season's ending whispers
the road has been empty for a long time
beneath a bridge a figure meditates at the water's edge
prince, real life runs in your veins!
You had only to turn death
to burning earth beneath the master's blue sheet
why does the uneasiness cease?
Neither your race nor your tears make you fruitful
you dry up between the seasons
it has not rained for ages
the tree is dying and the wind modulates grief
the day is over
the angels eluded the crowd of mockers
now their grief brings the landscape to life
with the women's grief as they bend to the opposite bank

PRELUDE 2

Cupids and naiads observe you with indifferent curiosity
— the fearsome watchman has been driven off
the husband can no longer do any harm
the frightened beast held for ransom
until another messenger appeases him
where are your eyes, keeper of the flocks?
The sacred bird fans out its tail as sole response...
how cool the sky is after the crime
spring light caresses the souls and the bluish horizon
of a naked old man at a young woman's breast
desire swells on the riverbank
o invisible lecher you invented it all
the cloak seems more alive than the body —
the bright-skinned one going off toward the clouds
turns his head to kiss the landscape where immortals and
        humans are gathered
truth hides within their bodies
for all are made of flesh and burning blood
desire enlivens every eye
the victim's blood is the victim's immortal soul
a finger points to it like a bouquet's homage to nipples of
        blonde young breasts
the city or the village waits for the remains
to be brought there at dusk
by the heartsick shepherdess

FUGUE 2

Sweetness retreated into a lament
you could imagine a series of tender sounds deep in a throat
love flows out when it no longer has an object
soon it will envelop the universe —
to have your own death come into view
is like emerging from a path and seeing

                                        a white mulberry tree
                                        at the foot of a rock
it stands out boldly against the stony background

                                        a bit gray a bit red
                                        a sort of cold pelt
so our own death
it makes itself known before the first sign of it
diminishes us
we leave each other   flow
with no goal but the most intimate shadow
you loved the love-object more than yourself
you were the love-object as a shadow of yourself
you will join the shadow under the mulberry tree
unite with death thrusting out —
there's the real storm on this earth
soon it will be the universe —

PRELUDE 3

Fear flew off with the last breath
now the wife sleeps and no one thinks of abducting her any longer
no one thinks of it yet
she has placed her head on the warm earth
her body too is nourished by it
perhaps Hamlet was right and she is dreaming
but perhaps her soul continues to keep watch and suffer
the suffering of farewells
caught in a vise between fear and unappeasable desire
which carries the infinite beneath a changing surface
perhaps she knows that it's up to her to cultivate her dark side
the tower did not carry out its duty as guardian
all nature showed itself indifferent
those bluish mountain ridges
the young ash tree and the beech
nowhere was there help for her
the farm in the valley's hollow barely opened
no god descended from the horizon…
was she loved only at that moment of burning breath
of blood congealed in all her limbs
Surprise rises in concentric circles
she cannot hear the grass rustling
she already has her two assassins

FUGUE 3

The landscape always precedes the story
the light on the south-facing slope the plateau and the motionless
    clouds
the walled town with its high tower
far-off buildings deserted squares
like eternally new ruins
around the mirror-smooth lake
the sheltering vegetation oaks acacias grass small flowers
that also adorn the spur of land at whose base a stream is winding
pride of a Mediterranean landscape!
Sweetness rises in tiers and spreads to flow back to our eyes
notes construct the landscape
blue and mother-of-pearl intoxicate the heights
but certain shades bring death's footsteps closer
the darker ones the yellower ones
there are other blues engendering dread
history devoured part of the landscape
it shone into the distance
to flow back like an echo blending with its source
to the rivulet of death where a dead man will tumble
certain blues become dumbfounded hands
without a definite plan no one understands anything
the witness's witness is present at another accident
hikers resting on an embankment, fishermen in their boat
feel here indifference there ignorance both seething outdoors

PRELUDE 4

The coming of spring will be celebrated on the wooded summit
    and in the clouds
— like a skiff where the daughter of the house pours ambrosia —
another god, like the nymphs and the naiads
or a flower born of misfortune…
a god consoles himself with a sad melody
once he loved without being loved in return
he had his love torn to bits
perhaps the child will bring him forgetfulness
and if he refuses it
joy will light up some corner of a humble heart
o shadowy bodies of the dying
there are little flowers and acanthus leaves around the wreaths
the foliage tricked the dying
they gave arms to death
their backs turned on so much love
what astounding music bursts out in the sky
the true victory is the sun's

FUGUE 4

There's no more question of anything but life
Oh joy of the sky after a long winter
the city dwellers have come out and decorate lawns in the park
with their flesh bleached by housebound retreats
each limb is resurrected
light fabrics were unfolded aired out
                                        perhaps washed in the stream
now they clothe bodies that seem luminescent
the foliage is precocious
as if the landscapes were painted
and the hand that acted on it was outside
instead of surging from the earth from roots from underground
      springs
games and conversations echo from the lawns
here and there an isolated figure is resting
dazzled eyes follow the clouds' movement
whose joy borrows from the floral blue on which they float
who is watching the houses?
Except for the temple and the neighboring palace they're all empty
naked bodies border the lake...
o freedom of the naked rock
attacked by the air to the point of dizziness
freedom from death that's been burned away
spread out on the grass like a sailor's ashes at sea
o woman draped in compassion's blue o graceful attendant to the
      earth's awakening!

Acknowledgments

The poems translated here were originally published in:
Ce qu'il y a à vivre (Editions de la Feugraie, 2013)
Sombre comme le temps (Editions Gallimard, 2014)
Préludes et fugues (Belin: L'Extrême Contemporain, 2011)

Some of the translations previously appeared in the following periodicals:
Poems 26, 38 (under the title "Forgive Them"), and 59 from Ce qu'il y a à vivre appeared in FIELD
Poems 1 and 2 (under the titles "God" and "Snow") appeared in Two Lines
Poems 26, 38, 39, 53, 56, 59, and 64 appeared in POEM (U.K.)
Poem 70 (under the title "Pisz na Berdyczow!") appeared in Plume (online)
"She Painted Artichokes," from Sombre comme le temps, appeared in Plume (online)
"A House and a Wall," "Meditation," and "Stones" appeared in Copper Nickel
"Dialogue" appeared in Two Lines
"Your Shadow" appeared in FIELD
"My Father, Me, and Everything Else" appeared in Plume (print anthology)
"Prayer," "A Stolen Dream," "Time in Color," "My Life," and "Portrait of My Friend" appeared in Plume (online)

Preludes and Fugues
Cycle A appeared in Modern Poetry in Translation (U.K.)
Cycle A, Preludes and Fugues 3 and 4 appeared in Crazyhorse
Cycle A, Prelude 2 and Prelude 3 appeared in Washington Square Review
Cycle B, Prelude and Fugue 3 appeared in FIELD
Cycle B, Prelude 3 appeared in The Wolf (U.K.)
Cycle B, Preludes and Fugues 1, 2, and 4 appeared in the Kenyon Review
Cycle D appeared in Cerise Press (online)

The FIELD Translation Series

1978 Eugenio Montale, *The Storm & Other Poems* (translated by Charles Wright)

1979 Vasko Popa, *Homage to the Lame Wolf: Selected Poems 1956-75* (translated by Charles Simic)

1980 Miroslav Holub, *Sagittal Section* (translated by Stuart Friebert and Dana Hábová)

Wang Wei, Li Po, Tu Fu, Li Ho, *Four T'ang Poets* (translated by David Young)

1981 Günter Eich, *Valuable Nail: Selected Poems* (translated by Stuart Friebert, David Walker, and David Young)

Benjamin Péret, *From the Hidden Storehouse: Selected Poems* (translated by Keith Hollaman)

1982 Miroslav Holub, *Interferon, or On Theater* (translated by David Young and Dana Hábová)

1983 Rainer Maria Rilke, *The Unknown Rilke* (translated by Franz Wright)

1984 Dino Campana, *Orphic Songs* (translated by Charles Wright)

1985 Karl Krolow, *On Account Of: Selected Poems* (translated by Stuart Friebert)

1986 Abba Kovner, *My Little Sister and Selected Poems* (translated by Shirley Kaufman)

1987 Vasko Popa, *Homage to the Lame Wolf: Selected Poems*, expanded edition (translated by Charles Simic)

1988 Judith Herzberg, *But What: Selected Poems* (translated by Shirley Kaufman)

1989 Anna Akhmatova, *Poem Without a Hero and Selected Poems* (translated by Lenore Mayhew and William McNaughton)

1990 Wang Wei, Li Po, Tu Fu, Li Ho, Li Shang-Yin, *Five T'ang Poets* (translated by David Young)

Miroslav Holub, *Vanishing Lung Syndrome* (translated by David Young and Dana Hábová)

Rainer Maria Rilke, *The Unknown Rilke: Expanded Edition* (translated by Franz Wright)

1991 Marin Sorescu, *Hands Behind My Back* (translated by Gabriela Dragnea, Stuart Friebert, and Adriana Varga)

1992   Novica Tadić, *Night Mail: Selected Poems* (translated by Charles Simic)

1994   Rainer Maria Rilke, *The Book of Fresh Beginnings: Selected Poems* (translated by David Young)

1995   Yannis Ritsos, *Late Into the Night: The Last Poems* (translated by Martin McKinsey)

1996   Miroslav Holub, *Intensive Care: Selected and New Poems*

1997   Attila József, *Winter Night: Selected Poems* (translated by John Bátki)

1999   Max Jacob, *Selected Poems* (translated by William Kulik)

2001   Vénus Khoury-Ghata, *Here There Was Once a Country* (translated by Marilyn Hacker)

2004   Eugenio Montale, *Selected Poems* (translated by Jonathan Galassi, Charles Wright, and David Young)

2005   Inge Pedersen, *The Thirteenth Month* (translated by Marilyn Nelson)

2006   Herman de Coninck, *The Plural of Happiness: Selected Poems* (translated by Laure-Anne Bosselaar and Kurt Brown)

2009   Emmanuel Moses, *He and I* (translated by Marilyn Hacker)

2011   Georg Trakl, *Poems* (translated by Stephen Tapscott)

2013   Pierre Peuchmaurd, *The Nothing Bird: Selected Poems* (translated by E. C. Belli)

2016   Emmanuel Moses, *Preludes and Fugues* (translated by Marilyn Hacker)